REACHING THE STARS

POEMS ABOUT Extraordinary WOMEN & GIRLS

JAN DEAN, LIZ BROWNLEE & MICHAELA MORGAN

MACMILLAN CHILDREN'S BOOKS

First published 2017 by Macmillan Children's Books
an imprint of Pan Macmillan
20 New Wharf Road, London N1 9RR
Associated companies throughout the world
www.panmacmillan.com

ISBN 978-1-5098-1428-2

1 3 5 7 9 8 6 4 2

A CIP catalogue record for this book is available from
the British Library.

Printed and bound by CPI Group (UK) Ltd, Croydon CR0 4YY

For the extraordinary Emma

Jan Dean

For Emmelie and Helena, and in memory of Deb Larcombe

Liz Brownlee

To the stars as yet unseen. Shine on

Michaela Morgan

Contents

A Girl Is Born	*Michaela Morgan*	1
Girls of the Week	*Michaela Morgan*	2
Girl Power	*Jan Dean*	3
Feminism Rules	*Liz Brownlee*	5
Sugar and Spice?	*Michaela Morgan*	7
Boudicca	*Jan Dean*	8
Khutulun, Mongolian Warrior Princess	*Liz Brownlee*	9
Fierce Woman	*Jan Dean*	10
QEI	*Jan Dean*	12
Song of the Match Girl	*Michaela Morgan*	13
Petticoats	*Michaela Morgan*	16
Stays	*Michaela Morgan*	17
Ask Eleanor	*Jan Dean*	18
Elizabeth Fry	*Jan Dean*	20
Marie Curie-ous	*Liz Brownlee*	22
Monster Maker	*Jan Dean*	24
Super Sisters	*Jan Dean*	25
Mary Kingsley's Adventure	*Jan Dean*	26
Fashion Parade	*Michaela Morgan*	28
Suffragette	*Jan Dean*	30
Marching Song	*Michaela Morgan*	31
Hunger Strike	*Michaela Morgan*	32

Amelia Bloomer, Suffragette Journalist, Fashion Reformer	*Liz Brownlee*	33
Edith Cavell	*Liz Brownlee*	35
Zitkála-Šá – Red Bird	*Liz Brownlee*	37
What Maria Montessori Thinks	*Liz Brownlee*	39
Miss Aylward's Journey	*Jan Dean*	40
For the Beauty of the Earth	*Liz Brownlee*	42
Amy, Wonderful Amy	*Jan Dean*	44
Undercover, September 22, 1943	*Liz Brownlee*	45
The Unknown Warriors	*Michaela Morgan*	47
Women's Work	*Michaela Morgan*	49
Anne Sullivan, Teacher to Helen Keller	*Liz Brownlee*	51
I Watch the Film of Helen Keller	*Jan Dean*	53
Viva Frida!	*Jan Dean*	55
Who Discovered DNA?	*Liz Brownlee*	56
My First Day at School	*Michaela Morgan*	58
Rosa Parks	*Jan Dean*	60
You Can't Just Point a Rocket at the Sky and Hope	*Jan Dean*	62
June 1963	*Jan Dean*	64
Paula Cain – Designs for Space	*Liz Brownlee*	66
Christa McAuliffe	*Liz Brownlee*	67
The Battle of the Sexes	*Liz Brownlee*	69
Gorillas in the Mist	*Liz Brownlee*	70

The Prize for the Most Books
  Borrowed from a Library Goes to
  Alia Muhammad Baker (Baqer)   *Liz Brownlee*   72
Fairy Tales   *Michaela Morgan*   74
Princess   *Michaela Morgan*   76
Advice to Rapunzel   *Jan Dean*   77
Choosing and Losing   *Michaela Morgan*   78
Malala   *Michaela Morgan*   80
Sara Pickard, Superwoman   *Liz Brownlee*   82
Tallulah Bryan – Inspirer of Kindness *Liz Brownlee*   83
The Black Mamba Squad   *Liz Brownlee*   86
I Am the Very Model of a Modern
  Girl from Planet Earth   *Liz Brownlee*   88
Heroines   *Jan Dean*   91
No Limits   *Jan Dean*   92
Tinker . . . Tailor   *Michaela Morgan*   93
Pillory Hillary   *Michaela Morgan*   94

About Jan Dean   97
About Liz Brownlee   99
About Michaela Morgan   101

A Girl Is Born

Here she is. She's small. What shall we call her?
Teeny? Tina?
Look at her toes, tiny strong and curled.
Ready to unfurl.
What shall she be?
A dancer?

Wow! What a noise – a bellow like an animal, loud
   and lusty.
Strong.
And her eyes blue as an ocean, and as deep.
What shall she be this newborn girl?
Her small hand waves.

Michaela Morgan

Girls of the Week

Monday's girl stands up proud.
Tuesday's girl speaks clear and loud.
Wednesday's girl likes to dream and ponder.
Thursday's girl loves to wander.
Friday's child can be slow – or speedy.
Saturday's child will help the needy.
But the child that is born on the Sabbath day
is as good as the rest in every way.

Michaela Morgan

Girl Power

All the women named in this poem are world-class athletes.

They said,   'You run like a girl.'
And I thought,   'Right. I'll be the speed of light,
    sprint fast as Dina Asher-Smith,
    or go a Paula Radcliffe distance,
    do marathons without assistance.'

They said,   'You throw like a girl.'
And I thought,   'Right. I'll fast-bowl out
            of sight,
    be Sana Mir or Katherine Brunt,
    keen-eyed and steady-headed
    as a panther on the hunt.'

'Can't catch,' they said, 'that's like a girl.'
'Yeah, right. Like Sarah Taylor keeping wicket?
Cricket balls fly faster than a roar of speeding cars.'
'Well, girls can't kick,' they said. I laughed.
'Tell that to Abby Wambach,
she could kick a ball from here to Mars.'

They said,   'You think—'
'Stop there,' I said.   'I've no more time to
                              waste on you.
   If you don't get it now, you never will.
   If women's strength and cleverness
   put your head in a whirl. Just pull yourself
      together,
   like a girl.'

Jan Dean

Feminism Rules

A feminist feels that women and men should be treated equally. For instance in the workplace, a woman should be paid the same as a man if she is doing the same job. It does not mean that you should be the same as a man. Many men nowadays could be called feminists.

There isn't a ruler
for measuring a feminist
you can stand up for your rights
and still want to be kissed
you can be a fashionista
and have a maths degree
be a model or mechanic
or love embroidery
a woman might be strong
but no one's perfect, not by far
working through your foibles
helps you find out who you are
feminism is a process
a conversation – fight,
things are complicated
often – there is no 'right'
ask questions of your own
of yourself and how you feel
no one has all the answers
if they do – they are unreal.

Believe in yourself, if someone
criticizes, disagree
being a feminist is just being
who *you* are or want to be!

Liz Brownlee

Sugar and Spice?

Sugar and spice and all things nice
That's what little girls are made of.

Burgers and fries, fails and tries
That's what girls are made of.

Strawberry ice creams, hopes and dreams
Plans and schemes, sliced green beans
Puds and pies, hopes that fly
Steel and silk, blood and milk
That's what girls are made of.

Michaela Morgan

Boudicca

When the Romans conquered Britain, Boudicca led
a rebellion against them. Her armies destroyed the
Roman cities of Colchester, St Albans and London.

Tall in my chariot,
bright as a sword,
my heart beats
like pounding hooves.

I will rise up,
with an ocean of spears, of arrows,
and fall on my enemies
like the iron sea.

I will fill the world
like bitter cold which bites the flesh.
And my enemies will hear my name
and fear me.

I will become the thunderbolt,
I will be the shaking of the earth,
the flood and tidal wave
that sweeps these Romans to their grave.

Jan Dean

Khutulun, Mongolian Warrior Princess

Khutulun was born around 1260, on the Mongolian steppes. Women had the same duties as men: fighting, horse riding and using bows and arrows. She helped her father repel the advances of armies led by the notorious Kublai Khan. She said she would not marry anyone she could beat at wrestling – but the trouble was she was just too good at it. In the end she chose someone she liked and didn't ask him to wrestle her.

Mongolian wrestler
Khutulun,
fought and won
against Kublai Khan.

A princess of
amazing forces,
she'd seize soldiers
off their horses.

Many suitors
came to meet her,
wrestling for love –
but none could beat her.

Liz Brownlee

9

Fierce Woman

Anne Bonny was a pirate in the Caribbean during the eighteenth century. The story told in this poem is true – she only escaped hanging because she was pregnant, and then she disappeared and no one knows where she went.

Anne Bonny was a pirate
Anne Bonny sailed the sea
Anne Bonny was a hell-cat
And here's her history.

Anne Bonny came from Ireland
From the fair town of Kinsale
She sailed in the crew of Calico Jack
And would fight with tooth and nail.

Anne Bonny crewed on black flag ships
And plundered where she could,
But Jack got caught and so did she
They all came to no good.

And back in old Jamaica
She's sentenced to the rope,
But Anne says she's a child inside
And where there's life there's hope.

So Captain Jack does dangle-dance
His toes tap on thin air,
But Anne escapes and disappears
And no one knows to where.

Jan Dean

QEI

Queen Elizabeth I was the daughter of Henry VIII and his second wife Anne Boleyn. The royal court wanted her to marry so that they would have a strong ruler, but she surprised them by being amazingly good at the job. She ruled well and wisely for forty-four years.

Here's the thing –
The blokes at the top really wanted a king.

Get what I mean?
They weren't keen on a queen.

So when it came to Good Queen Bess,
They thought that was an awful mess.

They thought a ruler must be male,
A girl in charge was sure to fail.

Elizabeth was no one's fool,
Under pressure kept her cool,

And proved a woman really could
Rule well and wisely. She was good.

She reigned alone, in power supreme.
A great and famous English queen.

Jan Dean

Song of the Match Girl

One of the nineteenth century's best-loved stereotypes is that shivering waif the match girl. As well as selling matches, girls (as young as nine) and women made the matches in conditions that led to them losing their hair, their health and their lives. The phosphorus on the white tips of the matches was responsible for a deadly condition known as phossy jaw. In London in 1888, girls and women employed in Bryant and May match factory went on a historic strike to protest against their horrific working conditions. This poem tells their story.

Life is no fairy tale
For a little match girl such as I.
Working all day from dawn to dusk,
Under a leaden sky.

'Course, I'm a big girl now. I'm ten.
So I work a fourteen hour day.
And *if* I don't get fined,
Five shillings a week is my pay.

But I *do* get fined. And so do my friends.
One by one we lose our pay.
For any little reason,
They take our cash away.

For dropping a match. Or a little laugh.
For any pause in a long long day.
For any tiny break,
They take our money away.

So strike, girls, strike!
Fewer hours! More pay!
And no more fines!
And safer work!
Listen to what we say!

We are a band of strong girls.
We keep our spirits high!
But the work we do is killing us,
And I'm too young to die.

My friends have yellowed skin.
Some have thinning hair.
And the unlucky have the phossy jaw,
Which makes the people stare.

That phosphorus is killing us.
It eats at us bit by bit.
What eats away at our skin and bone
Is that tiny white matchstick tip.

The tip is as white as a grinning skull.
As white as a winding sheet.
As white as the pus on an open sore,
White as the demon's claw.

It's as white as the ice in the bosses' hearts.
As white as the frost on their souls.
As white as the spirits that howl in the night,
Who wail to the world their woes.

So strike, girls, strike!
Shine a light to the rest of the world.
Fight the fight, strike a light,
Show them what we are worth.

Strike, girls, strike!
Fewer hours! More pay!
And no more fines!
And safer work!
Listen to what we say!

Michaela Morgan

Petticoats

They sound light
So pretty, so petty
But the hard facts are
They are heavy.

For respectability I can wear up to six at a time.
They give me greater grace. Make me look weightless.
I am fragility, floating. I am delicacy dancing.

I tote this weight of delicacy everywhere I go.
So hot in the heat. So wild in the wind. Walking is
    weightlifting.
My clouds of petticoats soak up the rain, drag me
    down.
Keep me in when I want to go out.
Snow is a no go. So, no, no. I just look at it from afar.
So white, so fragile. Light as feathers.

Whatever the weather my petticoats will sully and
    sulk.
So I stay still and sew. Stitching new decorations for
    my petticoats.
The sofa is the place to be. So far and no farther.
The place for me.

Michaela Morgan

Stays

They call them corsets
Or 'stays'.
And stay is what you must do when
    wearing them.
Stay.

Stay upright.
Stay quiet.
Stay still.
No room to breathe.
No air to run or shout or laugh out loud.

Contained, obedient.
Good girl!
Stay!

Michaela Morgan

Ask Eleanor

About 150 years ago, Eleanor Ormerod was a world expert on insects. She was self-taught and invented ways of getting rid of insect pests. In 1889 the American government asked for her help when national stocks of flour were infested with caterpillars. Their own scientists couldn't solve the problem, but Eleanor Ormerod did.

If it creeps or it crawls
in cracks in the walls,
if it's wormy and wriggles,
hairy-tickly as giggles,
if it's beetles or flies,
with wings soft as sighs,
or has composite eyes
and a sting-tail surprise,
but you don't know its name
– which is rather a shame –
ask Eleanor.

Are bugs eating the best
of your veg? That's a pest.
Are there holes in your vest
where the moths come to rest?

Are you feeling distressed
by a small biting guest?
Are you itching to blame it,
but can't really name it?
Ask Eleanor.

What is eating your rafters,
with floorboards for afters?
What's munching your chairs
and the treads of your stairs?
The roof will come tumbling,
the walls will fall crumbling,
but you can't recall
what started it all?
Ask Eleanor.

For Eleanor knows
what's destroying your rose,
knows wasps and knows weevils
and all of their evils.
Maggots and grubs
that feast on your shrubs
are all known in full.
No, bugs are not dull . . .
Ask Eleanor.

Jan Dean

Elizabeth Fry

More than 200 years ago, Elizabeth Fry was shown the horrors of Newgate Prison by a friend. She worked tirelessly to change the way prisoners were kept and treated. She also worked with the homeless and opened a training school for nurses. When Florence Nightingale went to nurse wounded soldiers in the Crimean War, she took 'Fry Nurses' with her.

When something evil meets our eye,
we often blink and pass on by,
we shake our heads, feel sad and sigh,
sometimes we're moved enough to cry,
but hardly ever do we try
to change things.

Elizabeth heard cries and wails
and weeping in the Newgate jail,
saw children's faces, thin and pale
and fearsome sights to make you quail.
She knew she really must not fail
to change things.

For prisoners are people too,
not creatures in a dreadful zoo,
or monsters in some demon crew,
but human beings through and through.
Elizabeth knew that this was true.
She changed things.

She fed the poor with soup and bread,
brought hope where once was only dread,
spoke up for kindness, bravely led,
showed that heart should work with head.
'Take courage. Don't fear truth,' she said.
Elizabeth. She changed things.

Jan Dean

Marie Curie-ous

Marie Curie was born Maria Sklodowska in 1867 in Poland. She went to Sorbonne University, Paris, when she moved in with her sister. She was fascinated by physics, and when she met her husband, Pierre Curie, she began working with him looking into the invisible rays given off by the newly discovered uranium. Marie realized there was something even more radioactive than uranium in the mineral samples she was studying. Both Marie and Pierre suffered ill health from their study of radioactivity, and it contributed to Marie's eventual death.

If something was radioactive,
would you want to find out why?

Scientists like Marie Curie
are curious – they have to try.

'There's nothing in life to be feared,
just understood,' she said.

But didn't realize the danger
would mean ill health ahead.

She spent long hours toiling,
with hands inflamed and raw,

found polonium and radium,
both unknown before,

which helped begin the search
for the world's most wanted answer –

a radioactive treatment
to help with a cure for cancer.

Liz Brownlee

Monster Maker

One of the world's most famous scary monsters was invented by a girl. Mary Shelley was eighteen when she wrote *Frankenstein* whilst on holiday in Switzerland. It was published in 1818, when Mary was twenty.

On holiday beside a wide blue lake
where water sparkles
and high mountains shine in sun,
three people think up stories just for fun.

The place is lovely – swans glide by
castles are mirrored in the calms
and Mary watches, dreams . . .
not at all the simple tourist that she seems.

This girl's imagination's huge and fine.
The story that she writes is *Frankenstein*.

Jan Dean

Super Sisters

The Brontë sisters wrote many famous novels, but they were first published under 'pen names'. Their books would not have been taken seriously if people had known they were written by women, but once they were accepted as great books the sisters stepped forward and revealed their identities. They changed how the world saw women writers.

Charlotte, Emily and Anne
Each faked the ID of a man
In order for their books to sell
Were *Currer, Ellis, Acton Bell.*

But when the books shot them to fame
They owned up to their proper names.
And everyone admitted then
That girls could write as well as men.

Jan Dean

Mary Kingsley's Adventure

Mary Kingsley lived in Victorian times and did all the things described in this poem. Explorers at that time often did not value the cultures they 'discovered' – Mary was unusual because she did not automatically think her British ways were always best.

An education's wasted on a girl
I've heard that said a hundred times
or more.
A girl should stay at home
and be a comfort to her mother . . .
I hope I was a comfort
for I loved my mother,
nursed her for years and years –
my father too, when he fell ill.

They died
within a few weeks of each other.
So, suddenly, my life was empty.
The pattern of my days ripped up.

I could have settled
in some English town
or looked, a little late,
to find a husband
a widower maybe?

Instead I came to Africa
And faced down everyone
who raised an eyebrow
at a woman travelling alone.

I loved it. Learned to fend
in jungles, lived among the people
took their sensible advice.

The life and ways of Africa
were strange to me
and wonderful.
I long for you to understand
this truth.

But Africans are not like us . . .
I can hear them now, those voices.

But 'different' does not mean 'worse'.
Time and time again I said it.
I insisted
like a dripping tap.

Changing minds
is not a minute's work,
but drops of water
wear away a stone . . .

Jan Dean

Fashion Parade

Welcome to the World of Fashion
and now . . . On With the Show

Here we have Emily
Wearing a splash of colour
With her sash of colour
Green, White and Violet.
She says, 'Green is for Give
White is for Women and Violet is for Votes.'
She who wears, dares!

And here we have Cordelia
Modelling the corset.
It fair takes your breath away!
Admire the tiny waist, the breathtaking shape, the
    perfect posture.
Accessorize with smelling salts and a sofa or chaise
    longue.
It's a cinch!

And here's Caroline
In her crinoline.
Oops watch your step!
Like a well-guarded snail Caroline can carry her cage
    with her everywhere.

The wire frame is so much lighter than the six
  petticoats she used to wear.
It's a sweeping success!

And here, taking her time to teeter on to the stage,
  we have Hu.
Hu. It's Chinese and means Tiger. And like a Tiger
  our lovely model is crouched –
But she won't be springing anywhere. She's far too
  dainty!
Look at her beautiful blood-red shoes!
Three inches in length for the tiny footed Hu.
A trained and tied foot makes a beautiful and dutiful
  wife, for life.
Someone help her to walk off the stage please.
Don't you agree she's been beautifully stitched up?

And who's next?
What's new?
Someone's coming – oh it's YOU
What will you wear?
What will you do??

Michaela Morgan

Suffragette

The suffragette movement started in Manchester in 1903 when Emmeline Pankhurst formed the Women's Social and Political Union. At first there were only six members, including the Pankhurst sisters, but the group became a powerful political force, and women eventually won the right to vote.

I want to make my own choice.
I need to use my own voice.
I won't be silent, won't ignore important things –
the world has queens as well as kings.

And so I march, protest and claim my right
to take part in my country's life.
I want what's fair – to have my say
on who makes laws and who holds sway.

I am no fool. I am no clown.
I won't give up. I won't back down.
If threatened, I won't run or hide,
I'll win this battle. I'll not be denied.

Times are changing.
Everyone take note –
women matter just as much as men,
and just like men we're going to have the vote.

Jan Dean

Marching Song

(or what the suffragettes may have sung)

1 2 3 4
We all count and that's for sure.

5 6 7 8
Time to influence the state.

9 10 11 12
Stand up, speak up for yourselves.

A dozen of us. Hundreds more.
Here to tell you what's the score.

Turn the tables, count our votes too.
You know it is the thing to do.

March along. Sing and shout.
Count on us. Don't count us out.

Michaela Morgan

Hunger Strike

Born with a silver spoon in her mouth,
to a life of tinkling teacups. Small talk.
There were things she wanted to say, but felt gagged.
So she sat still, waiting for the tea to arrive.
Aproned and capped, they brought it in.
A stiffly suited man to supervise.

It was another life. A week ago. A lifetime ago.
Now, in her prison cell, she sits and waits.
Hears the trolley approaching tinkling, clinking.
Here they come, capped and aproned. Another aloof
    man takes charge.

She sees a jug of milk held aloft.
And tubes.
Strong arms hold her down. Tubes forced down her
    throat.
She gags.
Dinner is served.

Michaela Morgan

Amelia Bloomer, Suffragette, Journalist, Fashion Reformer

Fashionable clothes for women in the 1800s were extremely heavy, and consisted of very tight corsets and many layers of woollen petticoats and skirts, which trailed on the ground. These clothes not only prevented women from taking part in many activities, but they were harmful to their health. Corsets squeezed internal organs out of place so badly that surgeons could not teach anatomy from a female body. Amelia Bloomer, an American women's rights advocate, was the first woman to suggest and popularize widespread wearing of loose tops over short skirts and the long, thin cotton trousers that became known as bloomers. It still took many years before all women were able to leave their confining clothes behind.

Amelia Bloomer
(who campaigned for votes)
didn't like corsets
or petticoats.
What did she advocate?
I think you can guess.
Bloomers! Blooming marvellous
freedom of dress.
And women all over
said what's not to like?
We can't ride in long skirts
on new-fangled bikes,

we can't walk very far
or breathe deeply or sing,
blooming marvellous bloomers
are wonderful things,
if you want to bloom
and work for your wealth
stand up for your health,
stand up for yourself.
How will you do this?
I think you can guess.
Wear bloomers! Blooming marvellous
freedom of dress.

Liz Brownlee

Edith Cavell

Edith Cavell was matron of what became a Red Cross hospital in Belgium during World War I, treating the wounded from both sides. As German troops advanced, some Allied soldiers were trapped. Nurses were not allowed to help, but Edith Cavell gave shelter to about 200 soldiers and, with underground workers, aided their escape to a neutral country. She was betrayed by one of the soldiers, tried, and shot on 12 October 1915. Before she died, she said, 'I realize that patriotism is not enough. I must have no hatred or bitterness towards anyone.'

A heart continues beating,
in peacetime and at war,
as a nurse continues caring,
it's what a nurse is for.

I can't take sides, and if you're hurt,
in this invaded land,
your battle wounds need tending,
your hands rests in my hand.

I must help these allied soldiers,
who are trapped, and so afraid,
my heart – it knows these souls
must be given shelter, aid.

Know this, though you betray me,
I've no fear, and on my part,
no hatred and no bitterness;
I freely give my heart.

Liz Brownlee

Zitkála-Šá – Red Bird

Gertrude Simmons Bonnin was born in 1876 in Yankton Indian Reservation in the US to a Sioux mother and white American father. She was sent away as part of a missionary experiment that took Sioux children and educated them in a boarding school. Here they cut off her beautiful hair, which in her culture labelled her a coward. The missionaries claimed to be giving them an education, but she could see that in fact they were aiming to strip them of their cultural identity and integrate them into American society. Red Bird became a talented violinist and teacher, and was the first Native American woman to publish stories derived from oral tribal legends. Her life became devoted to trying to fight for Native American Indian rights. Eventually she formed the National Council of American Indians to lobby for rights to American citizenship and civil rights. She took the name Zitkála-Šá to assert the identity of her roots.

You take your retribution
against my people now

for our Little Bighorn victory
but this I will avow –

my spirit will rise stronger
though you take my hair

to settle us in reservations
and take our freedom is unfair

I see your education
is to take my 'self' away –

you can give me English words
but cannot say what I can say

I will write of birds, and beasts,
the culture of my race

I will fight your slurs and lies
while I look you in the face

Stripped of my bark and branches
I will stand tall as a mast

In Government I'll fight our cause
get justice for us at last

I will stand against oppression
and threats, whoever you are

No one else defines or names me,
I name myself – Zitkála-Šá

Liz Brownlee

What Maria Montessori Thinks

Maria Montessori never let society's restrictions stop her from doing anything she wanted. She insisted on going to an all-male school, and against all odds became the first woman doctor in Italy in 1896. Gradually she became more interested in teaching than healing, and founded the Montessori Method of education, a child-centred educational approach based on scientific observations of children from birth to adulthood. Today, Montessori schools are famous worldwide.

Set children on a path to walk
give them letters, sticks of chalk
wooden blocks, let them build
see their hands becoming skilled
they will show a smaller friend
practise what they've done again.
They need to move to know each thing
that way the learning goes right in.
If their tools are beautiful
their play will be more pleasure-full
they need to look, touch, smell, and taste
let magic come at their own pace
make it fun, each hour they spend
they'll never want the path to end.

Liz Brownlee

Miss Aylward's Journey

Gladys Aylward was a Christian missionary running an orphanage in Yangcheng, China. In 1938 the Japanese bombed Yangcheng and then invaded. The children were in great danger so Miss Aylward led them on mountain paths to safety. When they arrived she collapsed (seriously ill with typhus fever), but she had saved all the children.

Now that clouds have covered up the moon
the mountain's black,
one hundred children huddle in the rocks
like sleeping sheep

and I'm their shepherd
on this long hard haul,
higher and higher by sharp crags,
creep-clinging
on the lips of deep ravines.

Escaping from the soldiers,
who have overrun Yangcheng,
now in this barren place
it seems to me
that we have leapt
from frying pan to fire.

I keep watch for wolves
and men with guns.

After twelve days walking
we reach the Yellow River.
There is no way to cross.

We kneel here
and pray for help.
We sing.
God's ears that day
are on a Chinese officer,
who hears us,
rides over, sees our difficulty,
and solves it with a boat.

In the city of Sian
there's safe haven
for us all. The children fall
into real beds,
and I fall into fever –
delerium
of terrifying journeys,
rockfalls, raging rivers,
dangers in the darkness
of the hidden moon.

Jan Dean

For the Beauty of the Earth

Rachel Carson was born in 1907 in America. She gained a masters degree in zoology from Johns Hopkins University, and went on to a job with the US Bureau of Fisheries (now the Fish and Wildlife Service). She wrote a groundbreaking, poetic book using the scientific names of creatures, but telling the stories about their lives with real facts. Her second book became a bestseller. She went on to write *Silent Spring*, an extraordinarily forward-thinking book about the dangers of poisoning insects and crops – it, too, was a bestseller, and helped get a very poisonous chemical, DDT, banned. Her writing sparked the beginning of the environmental movement.

She wrote with love
of all creation,
the need for nature
conservation,

she showed that
nature is a ring,
relying on every
living thing,

warned widespread
spraying of insect pests
killed not just pests
but all the rest

imagine this –
a silent spring
no creature stirs
and no birds sing

the bees don't buzz
no flowers thrive
she warned that
any left alive

would be pests like
caterpillars
that needed much
more toxic killers

Rachel Carson,
scientist,
the world's first
environmentalist

Liz Brownlee

Amy, Wonderful Amy

Amy Johnson was the first woman to fly solo from the UK to Australia and the first woman to hold a ground engineer's licence (so she could fix her plane as well as fly it). In the Second World War she flew in the Air Transport Auxiliary. In 1941 she and her plane were lost on a mission. 'Amy, Wonderful Amy' is the title of a song celebrating her flight to Australia.

Amy Johnson has no grave
her bones lie in the sea
though once a pilot of the air
flew high   flew wide   flew free.

The snow was falling on the waves
the current strong and icy cold
when Amy and her plane were lost
where channel breakers moaned and rolled.

They once sang songs for Amy
a flier of great fame –
a woman of great courage
remember Amy's name.

Jan Dean

Undercover, September 22, 1943

Born in France, 1914, to English parents, Pearl Witherington, who worked for the British embassy, moved with her family back to England when the Second World War broke out. She was an extremely determined woman and, frustrated by her civilian role, she applied to Britain's Special Operations Executive and was accepted. During her training she was greatly admired for her cool, resourceful nature, amazing them by being the best shot they had ever seen in the service. She received an MBE in 1945 and a CBE in 2004.

Parachuted into France,
resolved, courageous, calm,
to carry coded messages,
ammunition, arms.

Joined allied secret forces
attacked eight hundred times,
a bomb, a bullet in the side
of the German lines.

Soon, there was a million
franc bounty on the head
of this Network leader –
and a thousand German dead.

Cool, resourceful, clever
completely brave, though shy;
the best shot in the service –
Pearl Witherington, female spy.

Liz Brownlee

The Unknown Worriers

They kept the Home Fires Burning,
Painted on a lipstick smile,
Soothed the young and frightened,
Kept the old alive.

Some embroidered truth
And darned the damage too,
Stitched those silver linings,
Waved, while others flew.

They called, they stirred, they kept their post,
Tended hearth and hope.
Sent treats of socks and chocolate.
Wrote letters – and kept note.

Stoked the fires, kept the light,
Stroked cares and fears away.
Swept doubts and dust beneath the mat
To keep despair at bay.

Eyes bright. Eyes dry.
They smiled, smiled, smiled.
Another day. Another night.
Another lonely mile

To trudge . . . to drudge . . . to hold . . . to heal . . .
to live life on the edge,
to mop . . . to mope . . . to cheer . . . to cope . . .
to promise and to pledge.

No medals made for such as these.
No cenotaph. No fame.
No statues and no fanfares.
No history. No names.

Michaela Morgan

Women's Work

A 'rubble woman' or 'ruins woman' (translated from the German *Trümmerfrau*) was the name for a woman who helped to clear and rebuild the German and Austrian cities which had been bombed, once the Second World War was over.

When there's trouble,
Mess and rubble
Who do you call for?
  MUM!

She'll sort it.
Kiss it better.
Soothe it, smooth it, mop it up.
They call it 'Women's Work'.

And, after that war,
When the ruins of cities lay heaped around.
Monuments toppled, schools shattered, homes
    blown to bits,
the dust settled and in they came
the women, and the girls.

The 'Rubble Women'.
They did their work.
Racking through the ruins, brushing away the
    bombs, ready to rebuild.

In a chain they worked.
Arm in arm with handheld tools.
Brick by brick they picked their way
Stone by stone, bone by bone,
Collecting up lost shoes, scattered clothes,
    abandoned toys, the town hall.

Hand to hand, arm in arm
With pickaxe, hammer and bucket.
No manpower or machines – but glad of gloves –
They did their women's work sorting, clearing,
    tidying, saving.

The cities are cleared. The country's rebuilt
No medals or monuments to them in this world.
Who were they these superheroes?
These ordinary women, these girls.

Michaela Morgan

Anne Sullivan, Teacher to Helen Keller

Helen Keller lost both her sight and hearing as a baby. She became very frustrated as a child until her family employed Anne Sullivan, who cleverly found ways to help her communicate. Anne was Helen's teacher and companion until she died – by then, she had enabled Helen get to college, learn to type, speak, get married, tackle issues such as women's suffrage, and write a book.

I started with the word for 'doll',
finger-spelling on her hand.
This child could neither hear, nor see –
how could I help her understand?

To fill the space for song and bird,
all that sound and light explain;
out of reach did not exist
and dark and silence had no name.

Until I spelled into her hand
under a pump – though deaf and blind,
the word for water and the water
flowed together in her mind.

That living word grew in her hands,
gave her ways to hear and see,
let in hope and joy and love
with words that set her free.

Liz Brownlee

I Watch the Film of Helen Keller

Her hand moves against her teacher's face
like a starfish suckering its way.
She feels for sounds;
her thumb finds the click and buzz of 'guh'
against the hard ridges of her teacher's throat.
Her fingers tickle to the fizz
Of 'mmm' and puff of 'buh'
vibrating in the soft flesh of lips.

I watch the film. Helen hooks a finger
lightly into her teacher's mouth
and suddenly I feel the warmth and wetness
of my own mouth, my own tongue . . .
imagine someone else's hand against my teeth.
How did that teacher stay so calm
when Helen moved across her?
How did she not just smack that hand away?

I watch the film and see a double bravery;
Helen's for years of struggle,
holding tight to the world with her fingertips,
discovering words through nets of skin and nerves;

her teacher's for those same years of never giving up,
for letting herself be a living map of sounds,
for letting her own body be the place
where Helen could escape from silence.

Jan Dean

Viva Frida!

Frida Kahlo was a remarkable Mexican woman
who overcame illness and injury to
become a groundbreaking painter.

When illness left her weak –
lopsided, one leg wasted,
did she use a stick to walk?
or move unsteady as a sailor
on a swaying deck?

Maybe . . . but not for long,
she battled back
went wrestling, boxed.
She understood that *ladylike*
was just another word for *prison*
just another word to tie her down.

A bus crash crushed her bones –
she lay in plaster
her body still as stone, her mind ablaze
and moving free as fire
that roars unfettered in a forest

her spirit was a flame
as bright as stars . . .
ah, Frida shone.

Jan Dean

Who Discovered DNA?

Rosalind Franklin, born in London in 1920, went to one of the few girls' schools that taught physics and chemistry, and then on to Cambridge, becoming a scientist. Despite the prejudice of her male peers, she worked as a researcher on DNA while at King's College London, taking the photo that proved its structure, but a colleague showed it to her rivals Crick and Watson. Watson, realizing what it meant, published this discovery without properly acknowledging Rosalind Franklin's work.

The wonder of the spiral,
the helix shape of DNA,

found from a photograph,
using techniques of X-ray,

a crystallographic portrait,
photo number 51,

with great beauty illustrates
the shape for everyone –

the code of life that shows
the extraordinary means

of how all things replicate,
how we pass on all our genes.

Who took this photo,
with such a claim to fame?

Not Watson and Crick.
Rosalind Franklin was her name.

Liz Brownlee

My First Day at School

14 November 1960. New Orleans, USA. Ruby Bridges, aged six, is the first black child to enter an all-white elementary school. She was escorted in by armed guards as protesters shout abuse at her.

I remember . . .
Momma scrubbed my face, hard.
Plaited my hair, tight.
Perched a hopeful white bow on my head,
Like a butterfly hoping for flight.

She shone my shoes, black, shiny, neat.
Another hopeful bow, on each toe,
To give wings to my feet.

My dress was standing to attention, stiff with starch.
My little battledress.
And now, my march.

Two marshals march in front of me.
Two marshals march behind of me.
The people scream and jeer at me.
Their faces are red, not white.

The marshals tower above me, a grey-legged wall.
Broad of back, white of face and tall, tall, tall.
I only see their legs and shoes as black and shiny as
     mine.
They march along, stern and strong. I try to march in
     time.

One hisses to another, 'Slow down it ain't a race.
She only take little bitty girlie steps.'
I quicken my pace.

Head up.
Eyes straight.
I march into school.
To learn like any other kid can.

And maybe to teach a lesson too.

Michaela Morgan

59

Rosa Parks

In 1955 Rosa Parks refused to move from her seat in the 'whites only' part of the bus. This was an important event in the American Civil Rights movement – fighting for equal treatment for black people.

she sorts the drawer
knives at the left
forks at the right
spoons in the middle
like neat silver petals
curved inside each other

the queue sorts itself
snaking through the bus
whites at the front
blacks at the back

but people are not knives
not forks
not spoons
their bones are full of stardust
their hearts full of songs
and the sorting on the bus
is just plain wrong

so Rosa says no
and Rosa won't go
to the place for her race

she'll face up to all the fuss
but she's said goodbye
to the back of the bus

Jan Dean

You Can't Just Point a Rocket at the Sky and Hope

Katherine G. Johnson, an African-American woman, was one of the 'human computers' described in this poem. She called that era 'the time when computers wore a skirt'.

You can't just point a rocket at the sky
and hope a passing moon will catch it.

You have to plan
and plot
work out which spot
to leave from
know the landing place
and where re-entry's going to happen.

You need to find the line
of flight
fine hone your calculations
speculations
will not do it
guesswork
only leads to messwork.

So whose great maths work
put the first men up in space?
Dozens of women
working out the numbers.

Before the world filled up with PCs
tablets, smartphones,
these women worked it out.

They did the maths
that took the human race
up into space.

Back then computers
had a human
female
face.

Jan Dean

June 1963

Valentina Tereshkova was the first woman to fly in space. (She'd told her mother she was going on a parachute course when in fact she was going to orbit the Earth.) The most famous photograph of her shows her smiling.

Valentina smiles
    From Vostok 6 the world looks fragile
    somewhere down there the Volga flows
    her father drives his tractor
    and her mother's working in the cotton mill.

Valentina smiles
    Fills in her logbook
    checks the instruments.
    watches the lovely earth
    as she revolves in steady orbit.

Valentina smiles
    ALONE for three days
    circling and circling our planet.
    The sky is black and full of stars . . .

Valentina smiles.
    We watch her on TV,
    millions of us see that smile
    and wonder what she's thinking.

Valentina smiles
    She dreams of parachutes
    round as the domes of jellyfish
    of diving through the sky
    borne up by curved white silk.
    She falls in love with space
and smiles.

Jan Dean

Paula Cain – Designs for Space

Paula Cain was a clothes fashion designer when she saw an advert by NASA asking for pattern makers to make space blankets for satellites. She loved space, and was a *Star Trek* fan and a good pattern maker, so she knew she just had to answer the advert. Satellites are exposed to extremes of temperature out in space, but only work properly at room temperature, so Paula makes them exactly fitted space 'coats' of a very light, shiny, silver material called mylar. This reflects the heat and protects from the cold, so all the delicate instruments stay safe.

Up above the world so high
a bright, new star shines in the sky –
a satellite is flying by

it circles Earth by day and night
through space-cold dark, the fierce sunlight
but needs its temperature just right

all its instruments could burn
or freeze each orbit as it turns
so to address both these concerns

Paula fashions with mylar
lightweight, fitted coats that are
designer clothes fit for the stars!

Liz Brownlee

Christa McAuliffe

These were the things that Christa McAuliffe, who was a gifted teacher, believed in. Born in 1948, she was the first female US civilian (i.e. not a scientist) to go into space. She believed that you should keep going to attain your goals as 'the moon was always in the sky'. Tragically she was killed aboard the Space Shuttle *Challenger* in 1986 when it exploded shortly after launch.

You are made of stardust,
you are the instrument and
tune,

your mind will take you anywhere,
can touch both earth and
moon,

so read and listen, speak and sing,
proclaim your thoughts, be
bold,

keep curious, keep on learning,
question what you are
told,

assess where you have been,
and ask where you're going,
why?

Don't worry how long it takes you –
the moon is always in the
sky!

Liz Brownlee

The Battle of the Sexes

Bobby Riggs, a 1939 tennis champion, unwisely
asserted that the female tennis game was inferior
and that a top female player could not beat him. In
1973, Billie Jean King, who fought constantly for
recognition and equality for women in sport, accepted
his challenge, determined to beat him. She felt it
would set the progress of women back fifty years if she
lost and affect all women's self-esteem. In front of a
worldwide television audience of almost fifty million,
she beat him easily. The match was called
'The Battle of the Sexes'.

Bobby Riggs, tennis champ,
said a woman couldn't
beat a man . . .

Billie Jean King, tennis champ,
in three straight sets, showed
a woman can.

Liz Brownlee

Gorillas in the Mist

Dian Fossey was born in America in 1932. She was interested in animals from a young age. After going to Africa, she realized she wanted to study gorillas. Eventually she raised enough funds to do so. She wrote the bestseller *Gorillas in the Mist* about the gorillas she studied, spending the rest of her life under very dangerous circumstances, fighting for the rights of the gorillas.

When Dian Fossey
fell in love
with gorillas
in the mountains
of Rwanda,
her life
was planned
among the trees.

Through their gentleness
of being,
their vulnerability,
and strength,
sprung like mountains
from the grasses,
and their food
of flowers and leaves,

she mapped their world,
in their story,
Gorillas in the Mist.
She was killed
fighting poachers
for their right
to exist.

Liz Brownlee

The Prize for the Most Books Borrowed from a Library Goes to Alia Muhammad Baker (Baqer)

During the Iraq War, Alia Muhammad Baker was worried that her library in Basra might be burned down when the US and UK troops invaded. She had been greatly affected when she read about this happening to another library when she was a child. She began to smuggle books out in her car after work. When the British troops did come, she asked for the help of a neighbour who owned a restaurant next door to the library – and they managed to get out many more books and stored them in the restaurant before distributing them among many helpful Basra citizens. Ms Baker's house was stacked to the brim with books. The library did burn down – but most of the books were saved.

Ms Baker was chief librarian
of a library most renowned,
and worried that her library
was going to be burned down.

It was war – she had to save
the ancient texts for history,
smuggled most out to her house
and hoped no one would see.

Borrowed thirty thousand books
safe from burning and attack,
at war's end, library rebuilt,
took all thirty thousand back.

Liz Brownlee

Fairy Tales

My life could be a fairy tale
A happily ever after
Wishes granted
Once upon a time sort of life

But . . .

. . . I'd have to snog a frog.
Lose a shoe
Give up my voice
abandon choice.

I'd have to
shed a thousand tears.
Snooze for a hundred years
And grow my hair (like a golden stair)

I'd have to be
lovely,
elegant,
light on my feet,
Winsome, dutiful, with a smile so sweet.

Be meek and mild.
Never run wild.
Never be a mess.
Always wear the dress
And . . . of course . . .
. . . Be in distress.

So, if the fairy-tale life isn't all it's cracked up to be
Maybe try a magic sprinkling of . . . sweet reality?
The real world's out there with plenty of choices
for those with the courage, the heart and the voices.
No need for a tower, tiara or throne.
Time to make a fairy tale all of your own?

Michaela Morgan

Princess

Shy smiling
Hair tossing
Eyelash fluttering
Dainty stepping
Sound sleeping
Prince waiting
Happy ending?
Princess.

Michaela Morgan

Advice to Rapunzel

Sort yourself out.
    Don't hang around
    for someone else to rescue you.

Give yourself a trim.
    Pick up the scissors,
    it's not rocket science.

Make a rope ladder.
    Twist one. Plait one. Improvise.
    Use your head for more than growing hair.

Escape.
    Secure the ladder
    Shimmy down and leg it.

Don't look back.
    Get clean away
    Vamoose. Stay loose.

And learn your lesson.
    Staying put beneath a tyrant's thumb
    is dumb.

Jan Dean

Choosing and Losing

(a dipping rhyme for choosing friends)

Best friend,
Pest friend,
Better than the rest friend?
May . . . be . . . YOU!

New friend
True friend?
Help me when I'm blue friend?
May . . . be . . . YOU!

Close friend,
The most friend,
The one who likes to boast friend.
May . . . be . . . YOU!

School friend,
Fool friend,
Breaking every rule friend.
May . . . be . . . YOU!

Sporty friend,
Support me friend,
Sometimes rather naughty friend.
May . . . be . . . YOU!

Sharing friend,
Caring friend,
A daring and a scaring friend.
May . . . be . . . YOU!

Tidy, neat friend
Smiley sweet friend
Smelly feet friend
May . . . be . . . YOU!

Choose the best friends from the rest friends
   OFF WE GO!
Smarty, party, smiley, arty, sporty, naughty, caring,
     sharing, chatty, smelly or pest
   You're the BEST!

Michaela Morgan

Malala

Malala Yousafzai, born 12 July 1997, is a Pakistani activist known mainly for her defence of human rights and education for girls. On the afternoon of 9 October 2012, Malala boarded her school bus in the Swat district of Pakistan and was approached by a gunman, who asked her name and then fired three shots of a pistol at her head. She survived, recovered, and continues her fight for rights. She is now the youngest ever winner of the Nobel Peace Prize.

A girl with a book.
A girl with a book.
That's what has scared them –
A girl, with a book.

They get on to the bus.
They call out my name.
They aim. And they fire.
A shot to the brain.

Because a girl with a book,
A girl with a voice,
A girl with a brain,
A girl with a choice,

A girl with a plan
To have rights, like a man.
That's what they're scared of,
One girl, with a book.

A girl who has words.
A girl with a pen.
A girl to be heard
With support of her friends
Who want to live free –
That's what they fear,
A girl just like me.

Michaela Morgan

Sara Pickard, Superwoman

Sara Pickard is the embodiment of super-empowerment for people who have learning disabilities. She lives near Cardiff in South Wales. Sara has worked part-time for Mencap and now works part-time as a project officer on 'Hidden Now Heard', collecting the oral histories of people with a learning disability and staff from six former long-stay hospitals across Wales. She is a Trustee of her local Down's Syndrome Support Group and is also an elected councillor on her local community council. She is changing the prejudice of employers, and representing the capabilities of many disabled people. She has also toured as a professional actress in lead theatre roles.

Sarah loves to act and dance,
listen to music, swim,
she's played lead roles in theatre,
her heart soars when she sings,

she works part-time for Mencap,
helps run 'hidden now heard';
collecting long-stay patients'
histories in their own words,

her energy is boundless,
she's accomplished such a lot,
a real example of her quote:
'I've Down's Syndrome – so what?'

Liz Brownlee

Tallulah Bryan – Inspirer of Kindness

When Tallulah Bryan, then aged nine, watched a YouTube film about homelessness, she was so upset by it she decided to help homeless people herself. Helped by her willing parents, she set off into the streets of Leicester, UK, with a suitcase of warm clothes and a backpack full of food and drink. When the *Leicester Mercury* newspaper printed this story, hundreds of people's hearts were touched and they were inspired to help as well. Tallulah's family now run a breakfast club in Leicester Town Hall.

Are you cold?
Are you hungry?
Do you have no place to go?

Do your bones ache?
Is the ground hard?
Do your shoes let in the snow?

Are you scared
out in the darkness?
Do you have no food or coat?

Tallulah Bryan
has heard you cry.
She would like to offer hope.

And those who hear
about Tallulah
and her mission on the street,

giving food and clothes
and other help
to homeless people that she meets,

are inspired to
give themselves,
listening to those sad ordeals,

donating cakes
after a bake-off –
an Indian restaurant giving meals,

many people
knit warm clothes,
they need a large supply,

for when it rains
the homeless
have no place to go get dry,

a rough sleeper's
left the street
to a home for a new start,

Tallulah's kindness
is a light
that warms everybody's heart.

Liz Brownlee

The Black Mamba Squad

they
have
taken
your horn
the pride
of your nose,
that sharpens
and curves as
it slowly grows,
that guides your
calf and digs the
earth to find the
water to slake your
thirst, that gives you
identity, armoured and
bold, they've taken your
horn, for when it is sold,
powdered and packaged,
it is worth more than gold.
We are Black Mamba, anti-
poaching control, we guard
the animals, an all-female patrol,
a community unit, we're the counter-
attack, thoroughly trained in combat
and track, we will hunt you down, we
will find your snares, kill one of our rhino?
You will not dare, they are the heritage
of all Africans, we have no bullets, armour or guns
but we'll save the rhino for our daughters and sons!

Liz Brownlee

Poaching kills a rhino every seven hours in South Africa. The Black Mamba all-female anti-poaching unit is drawn from young graduates in the local community, who are trained in combat skills, given a uniform, and then guard the wildlife in their area, bravely patrolling the Kruger National Park unarmed. They are a visible police presence and deterrent and are proud to be protecting the rhino so that their children will still be able to see them. They have helped cut snare poaching by ninety per cent in their reserve.

I Am the Very Model of a Modern Girl from Planet Earth

I am the very model of a modern girl from planet
  Earth
photos documenting all the seconds I have lived,
  since birth
I've been inoculated for diseases that will paralyse
though burdened by my allergies I wheeze lots when
  I exercise
I'm tested till I'm dizzy in a manner most fanatical
so my maths is mathematical and writing is
  grammatical
with aid of a mnemonic I've recited all the elements
debated on philosophy to elevate my eloquence

I know that I can be most anything I have ambition
  for
but I've not any notion yet just what I have a mission
  for
but photos documenting every second I have lived
  since birth
show I'm the very model of a modern girl from
  planet Earth.

I could join up with the army dressing smartly up in
    uniform
be a novelist of fantasies and write about a unicorn
perhaps I'll save the planet with environmental
    vitamins
bring peace by meditation using transcendental
    disciplines
invent a new biotic that will cure all that's infectional
or lifelike human robot with an IQ most exceptional
compose a new world language just by using
    physiognomy
solve all our money problems rescuing the world's
    economy

I need to narrow options to decide between more
    easily
of all the possibilities that make my head spin
    queasily
but photos documenting every second I have lived
    since birth
show I'm the very model of a modern girl from
    planet Earth.

I could learn to dodge a question and be the next
    prime minister
or probe the paranormal and investigate the sinister
learn every definition in the *Oxford English
    Dictionary*
solve the power problem without using nuclear
    fission-ry . . .
find formulas for teaching the cantankerous more
    self-control
get rich by manufacturing a never-ending toilet roll
learn to sing a song so well my audience need their
    handkerchiefs
and then recite a poem quick to get it in before they
    leave . . .

I know that satisfaction is not who we are or where
    we're at
but how we live and how we love and all the blah to
    do with that
and photos documenting every second I have lived
    since birth
show I'm the very model of a modern girl from
    planet Earth.

Liz Brownlee

Heroines

Lara Croft
isn't soft
and isn't real . . .
but makes me feel
I could be dangerous and brave
inside a ruined temple
or a snake-infested cave.

Hermione Granger
is no stranger
to magic.
It's tragic
how little of my life's concerned with curses,
verses are more my thing, but still . . .
Hermione thinks.
She works things out.
And I believe if she can, I can.
I've no doubt.

Katniss Everdeen
best survivor ever seen.
Under attack,
bounces back.
When everything around me's going wrong
I remember Katniss
and feel strong.

Jan Dean

No Limits

After I have scaled a mighty peak
and swum a river seething with piranhas
I might paint my toenails shocking pink
or sew black bows upon my silk pyjamas.

Tomorrow I will bake a cake
and decorate it like a football pitch –
green icing and a sugar sculpture goal
before I chop down trees and clear a ditch.

I understand the loops of knitting,
I am good at babysitting,
I am a whizz at mathematics,
not scared of ghosts in creepy attics.

Maybe I will be an astrophysicist . . .
if that's the thing for me I will insist.

Jan Dean

Tinker ... Tailor

I could be a lawyer, a doctor, a teacher, a vet.
I could be a mother, an artist, or the pilot of a jet.
I could be the one who speaks up for a revolution
Or a steady force for status, calm, order, institution.
I could be a strutting model or a structural engineer
Or I could march in uniform to fight foe or fire or fear.
I could be a juggler ... a jeweller ...
What could be my scene?
Whatever it is, I choose to be
  A full-fledged human being.

Michaela Morgan

Pillory Hillary

For Hillary Rodham Clinton
Biog: super student, Governor's First Lady
(Arkansas), First Lady of USA, senator, Secretary
of State – and frequent target of criticism

verb: **pillory**; *historical* put (someone) in a pillory;
attack or ridicule publicly. Example: 'he found himself
pilloried by members of his own party'
First Lady: a woman who is married to a
president or ruler

Pillory Hillary
Call her a name
'Too pushy!'
'Too bossy!'
And more of the same.
Call her 'too wild'
Call her 'too tame'

Say she's a 'nobody, a 'nothing' – or she has WAY too
    much fame
'Just a good wife'
A 'prop', a 'support',
Or a 'harpy', a 'heretic'
A 'serious spoilsport'.

She's 'just a typical woman'
Nothing special or rare.
Or she's an 'atypical woman' – she's too different to
   bear.
Call her 'weak' if she whispers,
'Shrill' should she shout.
Call her out when she's in
And in when she's out.
She was a fine First Lady
Couldn't be beat
But now she wants power
Standing on her own feet.
So call her harpy, call her witch –
Call her *Lady Macbeth*
Call her hopes of the presidency
A waste of her breath.

Michaela Morgan

About Jan Dean

Jan Dean writes in a tucked-away space overlooked by two Clangers and a giant gerbil.

She has had two full collections of poetry published and is in lots of anthologies.

Jan is a National Poetry Day Ambassador for the Forward Arts Foundation and loves visiting schools to perform poems and have a brilliant time writing with children.

Website: www.jandean.co.uk

About Liz Brownlee

Liz Brownlee writes poems surrounded by books, looking out on to an apple tree full of birds, often with a cat in her lap, and her assistance dog, Lola, bringing her toys to play with, which is very distracting.

She has piles of poems in acres of anthologies, poems on the animal enclosures at Bristol Zoo, and her book of poems and facts about endangered animals is called *Animal Magic*.

Liz loves visiting schools, libraries, literary and nature festivals and organizing poetry events and retreats, and is one of the National Poetry Day Ambassadors for the Forward Arts Foundation.

Website: www.poetlizbrownlee.co.uk
Blog: www.lizbrownleepoet.com

About Michaela Morgan

Michaela Morgan writes picture books, novels, non-fiction and poetry. She spends some of the time living in the quiet countryside and some of the time living by the breezy seaside, and an enormous amount of time daydreaming, which is where so much writing starts.

Lately she has taken more and more to poetry, and often visits schools to perform and to run writing workshops. She is included in many anthologies in the UK and internationally and has another collection of poems, *Wonderland: Alice in Poetry,* also published by Macmillan.

Michaela hopes you enjoy meeting all the wonderful women and girls in these poems. Maybe you would like to find out more about them or write about one of your heroines.

Website: www.michaelamorgan.com